Changing Materials
Changing Shape

Chris Oxlade

www.raintreepublishers.co.uk
Visit our website to find out more information about Raintree books.

To order:
☎ Phone 0845 6044371
🖹 Fax +44 (0) 1865 312263
🖳 Email myorders@capstonepub.co.uk

Customers from outside the UK please telephone +44 1865 312262

Raintree is an imprint of Capstone Global Library Limited, a company incorporated in England and Wales having its registered office at 7 Pilgrim Street, London, EC4V 6LB - Registered company number: 6695582

Text © Capstone Global Library Limited 2009
First published in hardback in 2009
Paperback edition first published in 2010

Edited by Charlotte Guillan and Catherine Veitch
Designed by Ryan Frieson and Betsy Wernert
Picture research by Elizabeth Alexander and Virginia Stroud-Lewis
Originated by Modern Age Repro House Ltd
Printed in China by South China Printing Company Ltd

ISBN 978 0 431 17476 1 (hardback)
13 12 11 10 09
10 9 8 7 6 5 4 3 2 1

ISBN 978 0 431 17481 5 (paperback)
14 13 12 11 10
10 9 8 7 6 5 4 3 2 1

British Library Cataloguing in Publication Data
Oxlade, Chris
Changing shape. - (Changing materials)
531.3'82
A full catalogue record for this book is available from the British Library.

Acknowledgements

We would like to thank the following for permission to reproduce photographs: Alamy **pp. 6** (© Jorge Sanchez-Conejo), **9** (© Positive image), **13** (© Urban Zone), **21** (© David R. Frazier Photolibrary Inc.), **22** (© Chad Ehlers); Art Directors and Trip Photo Library **pp. 8, 12, 14, 15, 18, 23, 25** (Helene Rogers); © Capstone Global Library **pp. 4, 5, 16** (MM Studios); © Capstone Global Library Ltd. 2004 **p. 20** (Debbie Rowe); © Capstone Publishers **pp. 19, 26-29** (Karon Dubke); Photolibrary **pp. 10** (Digital Vision), **24** (© Odilon Dimier); Shutterstock **pp. 7** (© Stuart Miles), **11** (© Brian Chase).

Cover photograph of close-up of a woman holding colourful rubber bands reproduced with permission of Getty Images / © bilderlounge.

Every effort has been made to contact copyright holders of material reproduced in this book. Any omissions will be rectified in subsequent printings if notice is given to the publishers.

All the Internet addresses (URLs) given in this book were valid at the time of going to press. However, due to the dynamic nature of the Internet, some addresses may have changed, or sites may have changed or ceased to exist since publication. While the author and Publishers regret any inconvenience this may cause readers, no responsibility for any such changes can be accepted by either the author or the Publishers.

Contents

About materials 4

Changing materials 6

Stretching 8

Squashing 10

Bending and twisting 12

Investigating changing shape 14

Comparing materials 16

Soft and hard materials 18

Flexible materials 20

Rigid and brittle materials 22

Going back to shape 24

Solids, liquids, and gases 26

Which material? 28

Glossary 30

Find out more 31

Index 32

Words appearing in the text in bold, **like this**, are explained in the glossary.

About materials

How many different types of materials do you know? Can you see any wood, plastic, or metal in this photo? These are all materials we use to make things.

These things are made from several different materials.

Can you see a natural material and a material made by humans?

Some materials are **natural** materials. We get them from the world around us. Wood, clay, and water are natural materials. Humans make other materials, such as glass and plastic.

Changing materials

Ice changes into water when it melts.

Materials can change shape. Sometimes we can change the **properties** of a material. The properties of a material include how it looks and feels.

We can pull or push some materials to make them change shape. Some materials change shape easily, such as modelling clay.

Modelling clay changes shape when you pull it.

Stretching

When you pull on the ends of a piece of material it can get longer. Materials change shape when they stretch.

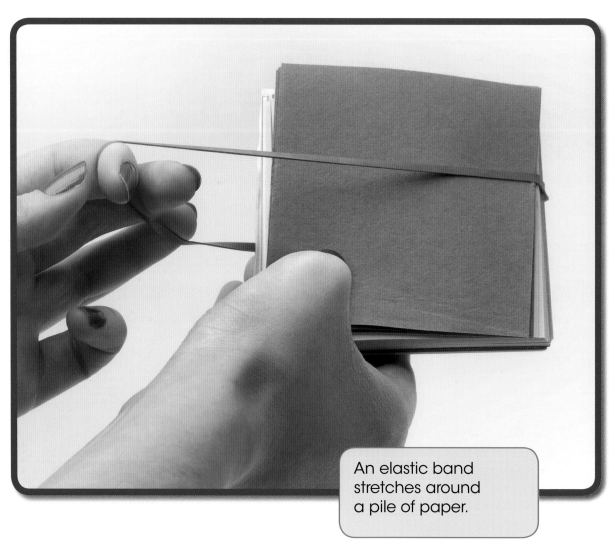

An elastic band stretches around a pile of paper.

Some materials are easy to stretch. When you pull them they get much longer. They get thinner when they stretch, too. Some materials such as stone do not stretch easily.

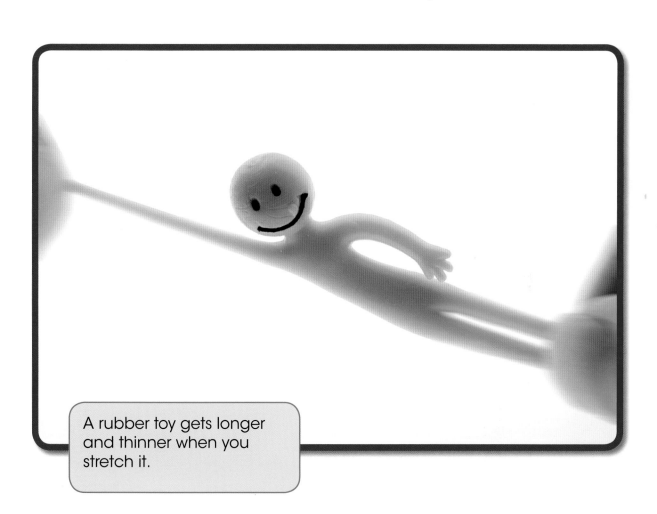

A rubber toy gets longer and thinner when you stretch it.

Squashing

When you push on the ends of a piece of material it can move. The material can be squashed. Squashing is a change of shape.

A bouncy toy squashes easily.

Dough gets thinner and spreads out when you roll it.

Some materials are easy to squash. When you squash them they get thinner. Some materials get shorter, too. Some materials such as glass do not squash easily.

Bending and twisting

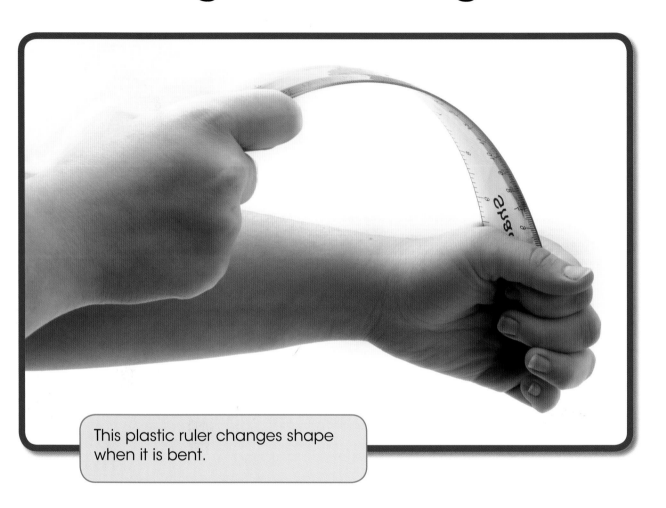

This plastic ruler changes shape when it is bent.

When you hold an object in two places and move your hands towards each other, you can make it bend. Bending an object can make it change shape.

When you wind the propeller of a model plane, you twist the elastic band. The elastic band changes shape.

Objects **twist** when their ends are turned in opposite directions. Twisting an object can make it change shape. Not all materials bend or twist easily.

Investigating changing shape

Try changing the shape of different materials. Try to stretch them, squash them, bend them, and **twist** them. Here are some materials for you to try:

Materials

A pencil rubber

A thin strip of wood

A plastic spoon

A china mug

Modelling clay

Is it easy to bend a wooden stick? Does it change shape?

Was it easy or difficult to change the shape of the materials you tested? Write down the **properties** of each material in a table in a notebook. Put the material in one column and its properties in another column.

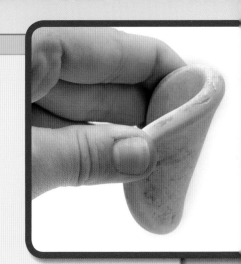

Material	Properties
A pencil rubber	It squashes, bends, and twists. It always goes back to the same shape.
A thin strip of wood	
A plastic spoon	
A china mug	
Modelling clay	

Comparing materials

On page 14 you **compared** how easily some different materials stretched, squashed, bent, and **twisted**. Here are some more materials that you might have tested. They are stone, glass, paper, and leather.

Can you identify the materials in this photograph?

This table shows some **properties** of the materials in the picture opposite. Did you **observe** some of the same properties in your own tests?

Material	Properties
Stone	It does not change shape.
Glass	It does not change shape.
Paper	It does not stretch. It bends and twists easily.
Leather	It stretches a little. It bends and twists easily. It sometimes goes back to the same shape.

Soft and hard materials

Some materials are soft. It is easy to change their shape. Modelling clay is easy to squash and stretch because it is soft. You can make it into any shape you like.

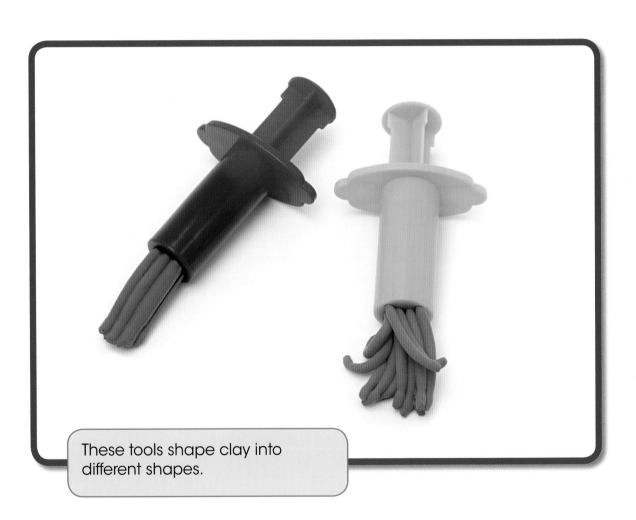

These tools shape clay into different shapes.

A metal knife cuts because it is hard and it does not change shape. You should ask for an adult's help before using a knife.

Some materials are hard. It is difficult to change their shape. For example, it is difficult to squash stone.

Flexible materials

Paper is flexible. We can fold it to make new shapes.

Some materials are easy to bend and **twist**. We use the word **flexible** to describe these materials.

Thin pieces of material are easier to bend than thick pieces of material. For example, you can bend a metal paper clip easily, but you cannot bend a thick metal rod.

The thin branches on these trees bend in the wind, but the thick branches do not.

Rigid and brittle materials

It is hard to make some materials change shape. They do not stretch, squash, bend, or **twist**. We use the word stiff, or **rigid**, to describe these materials. Stone and china are hard, rigid materials.

Rigid materials like bricks are good for building.

Breadsticks do not bend.
They are brittle.

If you try to change the shape of some hard materials, the material can snap. Materials that break like this are called **brittle** materials.

Going back to shape

A slinky spring always shrinks back into its old shape.

When you push or pull on a material to change its shape, then let go again, the material sometimes goes back into its old shape. For example, when you squeeze a rubber ball it changes shape, but it goes back into its old shape when you stop.

Garden wire stays in shape when you bend it.

When you push or pull on other materials they stay in the new shape when you let go. These materials are useful for making things. Modelling clay stays in the shape you make, so you can make models.

Solids, liquids, and gases

All materials are either **solids**, **liquids**, or **gases**. For example, ice is a solid, water is a liquid, and steam is a gas. Solids, liquids, and gases have different **properties**.

An ice cube is solid.

A liquid drink changes its shape to fill the bottom of a glass.

A solid keeps its shape unless something changes its shape. Liquids and gases change shape more easily. For example, a liquid will always spread out to fill a container, and a gas such as air will fill the whole of a balloon.

Which material?

We use different materials for different things. Here are two drinking cups. One is made from glass. The other is made from paper. Which would you give to a small child to drink from?

The paper cup would be best. The child could squash or drop the cup without it breaking. But glass is a **brittle** material and the glass may smash.

Here are two knives. One is made from plastic, the other is made from metal. Which one is best for cutting a material such as hard cheese?

The metal knife would be best for cutting a hard material. Plastic changes shape more easily. It would bend and **twist** as you tried to cut with it.

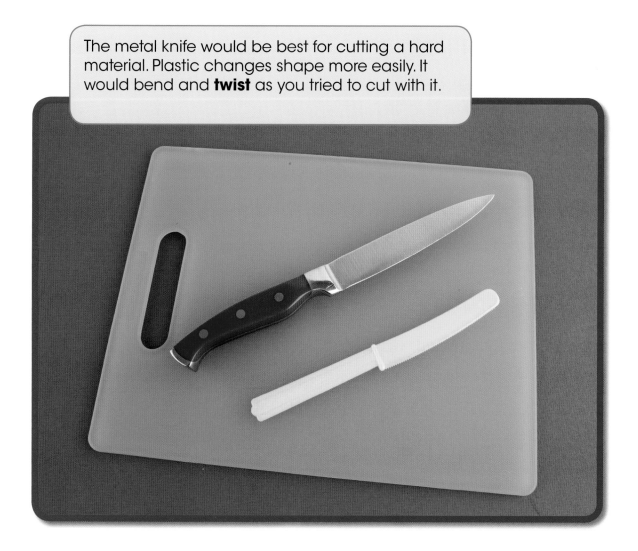

Glossary

brittle material that snaps easily when you try to bend it

compare look at the differences between two or more things

flexible material that bends easily

gas material that flows and fills a space. Air is a gas.

liquid material that flows and fills the bottom of a container. Water is a liquid.

natural something that is not made by people. It comes from animals or plants, or the rocks of the Earth.

observe look at something carefully

property things that tell us what a material is like, such as how it feels and looks

rigid material that does not bend or twist

solid material that stays in shape and does not flow. Wood is a solid.

twist push and pull on the ends of an object, making the ends turn in opposite directions

Find out more

Books

Check It Out: Materials, Clint Twist (TickTock, 2005)

Investigating Science: How Do We Use Materials?, Jacqui Bailey (Franklin Watts, 2005)

Using Materials series (*Cotton, Glass, Metal, Paper, Plastic, Rock, Rubber, Soil, Water, Wood, Wool*), Chris Oxlade (Heinemann Library, 2002)

Start-Up Science: Materials, Claire Llewellyn (Evans Books, 2004)

Websites

www.bbc.co.uk/schools/scienceclips

www.bbc.co.uk/schools/podsmission
There are fun materials activities on these BBC websites.

www.crickweb.co.uk/ks1science.html
Visit this website for interactive science activities.

Index

bending 12, 14, 29
breadsticks 23
bricks 22
brittle materials 23, 28

china 14, 15, 22

dough 11
drinking cups 28

elastic band 8, 13

garden wire 25
gases 26, 27
glass 5, 16, 17, 28

hardness 19, 22, 29

ice 6, 26

knives 19, 29

leather 16, 17
liquids 26, 27

materials
    changing shape 6–15,
        24–25
    flexible materials 20–21
    man–made materials 5
    natural materials 5
    properties 6, 15, 17, 26

rigid and brittle materials
    22–23, 28
soft and hard materials
    18–19, 22, 29
thick and thin materials
    11, 21
metals 4, 19, 21, 29
modelling clay 7, 14, 15,
    18, 25

paper 16, 17, 20, 28
plastic 4, 5, 12, 14, 15, 29
properties 6, 15, 17, 26

rubber 9, 14, 15, 24

slinky spring 24
softness 18
solids 26, 27
squashing 10–11
stone 16, 17, 19, 22
stretching 8–9

toys 9, 10
twisting 13, 29

water 5, 6, 26
wood 4, 5, 14, 15